MONSTER MATHS

MONEY

WRITTEN BY

MADELINE TYLER

ILLUSTRATED BY

AMY LI

BookLife PUBLISHING

©2021
BookLife Publishing Ltd.
King's Lynn
Norfolk PE30 4LS

ISBN: 978-1-83927-162-5

Written by:
Madeline Tyler

Edited by:
John Wood

Designed/Illustrated by:
Amy Li

PHOTO CREDITS

Tickles wants to buy her
brother, Pod, a present.

Pod likes monster sweets
and monster treats...
4

... and cuddly
monsters with
spiky horns!

Tickles has lots of coins.

Tickles has 5 growls and 8 rumbles.

These coins are round.

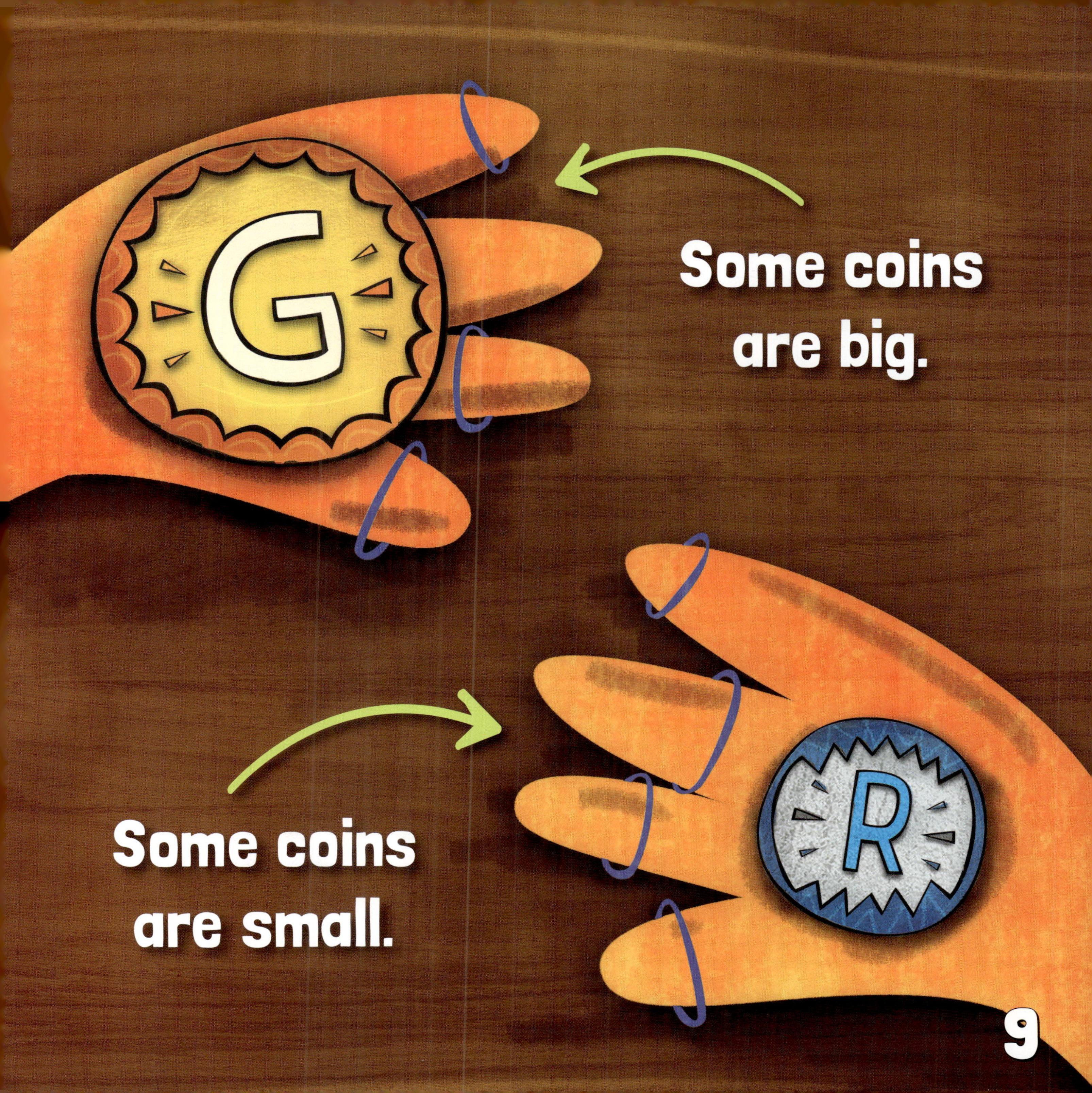

Some coins
are big.
Some coins
are small.

What shall she buy?

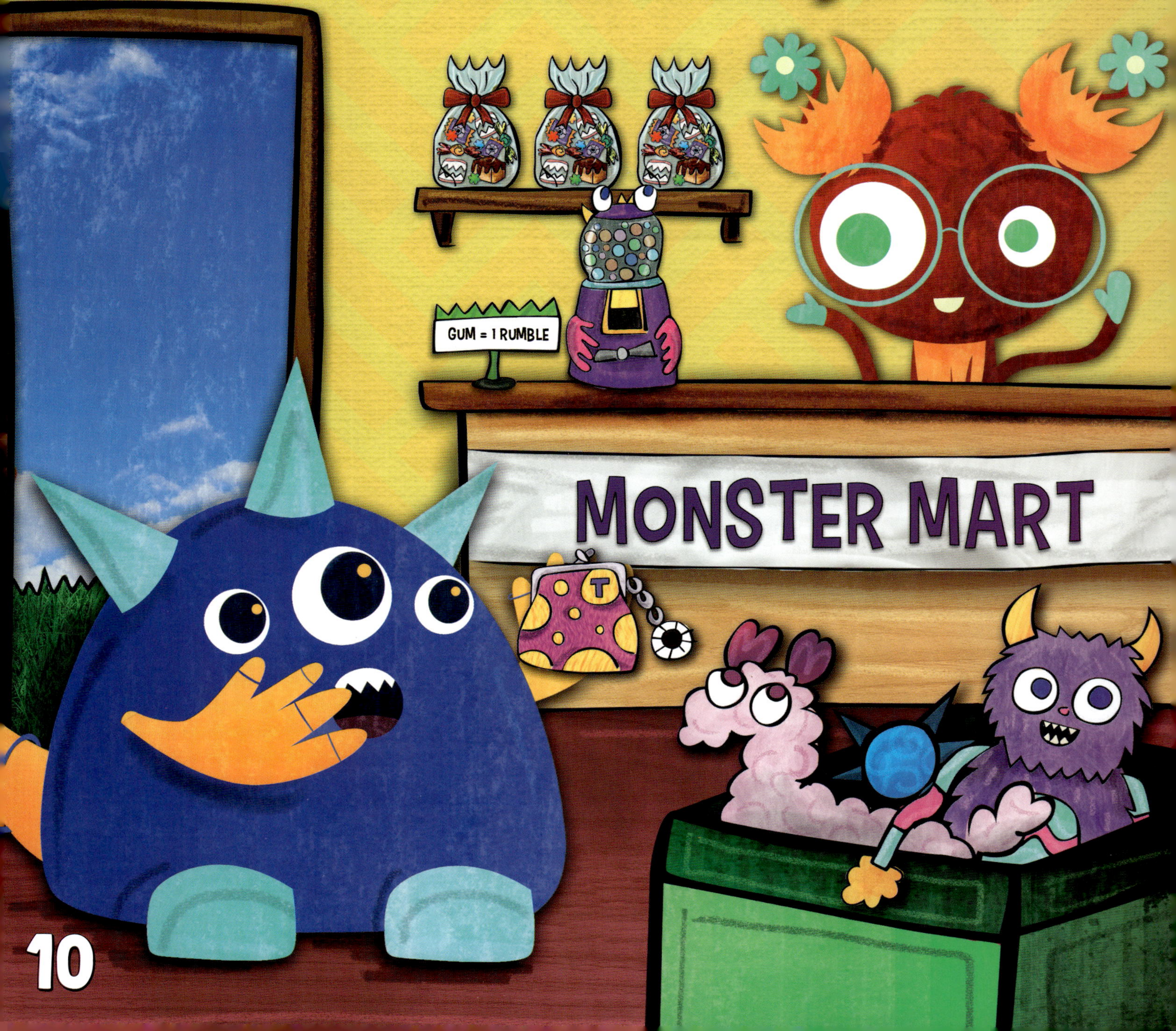

GUM = 1 RUMBLE
MONSTER MART

Monster sweets cost 2 growls and 3 rumbles.

How many growls does Tickles need?

How many rumbles does Tickles need?

Does Tickles have enough coins?

Yes, she does!
GUM = 1 RUMBLE
RT

But look – a cuddly monster!

Pod loves cuddly monsters!

This cuddly monster costs 3 growls and 5 rumbles.

Can you count the growls and rumbles?

$$1 + 1 + 1 = 3$$

$$1 + 1 + 1 + 1 + 1 = 5$$

Does Tickles have enough coins?

Yes, she does!
GUM = 1 RUMBLE
21

Tickles has spent all her money.

She bought monster sweets and a cuddly monster.

Pod loves his presents!
Well done, Tickles.